CELEBRATING THE HOLIDAYS
WITH JOSEPH & EMMA SMITH

PRICELESS GIFTS

GRACIA N. JONES

Covenant Communications, Inc.

Covenant®

Acknowledgments

Thanks to my dear friend Susan Roylance, whose enthusiasm and expertise made the creation of this book possible.

Thanks to Michael Ballam, who felt the spirit of this message and opened the way for it to be made available.

Special thanks to JoAnn Jolley, Valerie Holladay, and the production staff at Covenant.

Finally, thanks to my husband, Ivor, for his constant encouragement and the priceless gift of his love.

Author's Note

This book is written to provide inspirational reading for LDS people, young and old. While care has been taken to relate the historical events as accurately as possible, this book is not intended as an historical resource.

I have referred frequently to *The History of the Church of Jesus Christ of Latter-day Saints,* by Joseph Smith (with introduction and notes by B. H. Roberts). All sources are listed in the Bibliography at the end of the book.

The original spelling of quoted material has been retained, although some punctuation has been added for easier reading.

Cover painting *A Father's Gift* © Liz Lemon Swindle, Repartee & Foundation Arts

Interior illustrations, *Restoration of the Aaronic Priesthood, Emma's Hymns, Translation of the Bible, You Shall be a Comfort* © Liz Lemon Swindle, Repartee & Foundation Arts

Published by Covenant Communications, Inc.
American Fork, Utah

Printed in the United States of America
First Printing: October 1998

05 04 03 02 01 00 99 98   10 9 8 7 6 5 4 3 2 1

ISBN 1-57734-342-5

TABLE OF CONTENTS

LIST OF ILLUSTRATIONS

Introduction

For most of us, holidays such as Christmas, New Year's Day, Thanksgiving, and Easter—along with anniversaries and birthdays—are traditionally celebrated with festivities centered around giving and receiving gifts.

In fact, the commercial aspects of celebrating the various holidays are so ingrained in us that most of us could not imagine the holidays without the specific decorations of the season—trees, lights, chocolate-covered marshmallow Santas, and Easter bunnies. And who among us can resist indulging in shopping sprees justified by the "spirit of the season?" Notwithstanding all of this, after the wrapping paper and tinsel are swept up, we sense a certain emptiness—a longing not satisfied by the abundance of material gifts.

Considering this reality of modern life, I started wondering how the early Latter-day Saints celebrated Christmas, birthdays, and other holidays. I especially wondered what Christmas was like for my great-great-grandparents, the Prophet Joseph Smith, and his wife, Emma. It occurred to me that this man, who had personally communed with deity, would have something worthwhile to teach us about how to celebrate the Lord's birthday.

Encouraged by my friend Susan Roylance, I began to study the history of the Church, looking for any mention of how the holidays were spent. I soon became aware that in the founding years of The Church of Jesus Christ of Latter-day Saints, Joseph and Emma Smith did not appear to keep Christmas in the manner common to us today. Nevertheless, the fact that Joseph was a prophet did not prevent his family from enjoying simple holiday pleasures; these activities were simply much different from those of our day.

As I reviewed the *History of the Church*, which was taken from the writings of the Prophet Joseph Smith, I saw that very little was said of family and personal activities, including the celebration of traditional holidays and special events; his major focus was on the work of the Lord. For example, Joseph only occasionally commented on the passing of Christmas Day. However, as the old year came to a close and the new year began, he frequently took stock of his progress, setting goals for himself or the Church. Birthdays were occasionally mentioned, but nothing was said of birthday celebrations.

Emma herself left very little in the way of writing or discussion. I wish she would have written more. Lacking her personal input, we can only speculate on her activities on the holidays. She did, however, leave ample evidence that she believed her husband, and believed *in* him. The records show that she sacrificed all earthly comforts and security in order to help him further the work the Lord had given him to do.

As we remember that the Prophet Joseph Smith revealed a great deal about Jesus Christ—perhaps more than any other person who ever lived—we begin to realize the truly priceless gifts we receive through his efforts. These priceless gifts, as I have described them in this book, are just a few, among many, which could be mentioned— gifts that make possible a deeper and more personal understanding for each of us, of the Savior and his mission.

Earthly Treasures

Search though we may, we can find no mention of Joseph and Emma battling crowds to buy last-minute Christmas gifts. They undoubtedly did exchange gifts on birthdays, anniversaries, and holidays. Joseph once declared Emma to be the wife of his youth and the choice of his heart. And we know she loved him and she treasured the gifts Joseph gave her—an opal ring, a cameo brooch, the necklace of gold beads that she "always wore," even when the beads became so bent and worn through that she had to replace some of them with amber. These trinkets have been passed down in our family to be treasured for generations after she was gone.

Through the odyssey of their seventeen years together, the Prophet Joseph and Emma were not privileged to enjoy peace or the pursuit of their own happiness. In my study of Church history, I found that during some holidays Joseph and Emma were separated by miles; as Joseph traveled in his ministry, Emma was generally occupied with taking care of her family and an endless stream of boarders.

What were the holidays like for them?

To catch the spirit of their holidays, it is necessary to erase from our mind many elements typical of what constitutes a holiday celebration today. For instance, in their world during the years 1827 to 1844, there were no twinkling electric lights on a Christmas tree, or strings of colored lights across city streets.

We gain insights into what their family Christmas celebrations may have been like through reading in the history of their son, Alexander, who was my great-grandfather. The following excerpt, written by Alexander's daughter, Vida, gives an intimate view of how Emma's family members observed special days. Alexander's wife, Elizabeth, was an orphan from the age of six and was raised in Emma's home. Their memories of the early years under Emma's roof must certainly have stimulated their own holiday traditions and their value of cheerfully coping—whatever the circumstances, whatever the season. Vida's description of her childhood gives us a glimpse of what her parents both learned, as they grew up, in Emma's household:

> If we had fun we made it, and mother and father [Alexander and Elizabeth Smith] helped both in making and partaking. Our time was filled with duties, many of them hard and distasteful,

but life for a large growing family offers many opportunities for recreation, and we were taught by our parents a very good motto: "If you want to have a good time, always take one with you."

We were . . . thrown upon family resources for pleasures. It was well for us that father and mother were merry-hearted and had not forgotten the gladsomeness of their youth. . . . Our little trips to gather wild fruit, etc., were made the occasion of real festivity, and birthdays and holidays were luxuriously observed with an extra dinner, and the use of the prettiest dishes and table linen. . . .

Not often in our childhood years had Christmas failed to bring us something in the way of a gift. If it were ever so simple and poor it kept the season fresh in our hearts. . . ."

After Alexander and Elizabeth moved their family to northern Missouri, to farm, times were extremely hard.

For Christmas the closely-covered, "holed-up" potatoes were opened and a portion not quite perfect enough for seed potatoes [was] opened and . . . with much labor secured. This was a hazardous thing to do, for the aperture thus made through earth and straw could never be quite as close as before, and this means of cold storage was the one way of keeping family vegetables and apples, if one were fortunate enough to have them.

In this year but one man in the whole countryside had winter apples. His home was over a mile from ours, and the possibility of his parting with any of the treasures was very doubtful. But father started with a sack and a few pieces of money across the snowdrifts toward neighbor Jones. Thinking of it now, I can estimate the joy a good pair of snowshoes would have been on that and similar occasions. In vain the children clamored to know where father was going. Mother had had enough of Christmas without any secrets. She had one now and proposed to have her fun with it.

It was nearly dark when Father came slowly back looking like a veritable Santa Claus, with the frost on his brown beard, and the big bumpy looking pack on his shoulders, and never did old Santa's pack hold such delicious treat[s] as that half bushel of big, yellow, pink-cheeked apples were to the family in the farmhouse; and never was a short journey much harder than the one by which they came that day. (Vida Smith, *"Biography of Patriarch Alexander Hale Smith,"* RLDS Archives, Independence, Missouri; typed manuscript copy in author's possession)

The children of Alexander's family enjoyed the hand-carved game of "jackstraws," which consisted of twenty men, ten guns, five swords, and fifteen spears in each set. A hook made of a bent pin in a smooth piece of wood was given each player. The set of figures would be thrown on the floor. Each player took a turn trying to retrieve a piece without disturbing other pieces (which resulted in the loss of a turn). The winner was the one with the most pieces at the end of the game. For the boys in the family, whittling the parts for this game was as much fun as playing it.

They also enjoyed the game of "thumbs up," in which even the smaller children participated. Another favorite game was "Who Has the Button?" where a button is passed around the circle and finally dropped into someone's hands; one in the middle of the circle, who is "it," must guess who has the button. Such games, and the making of "angels" in the snow, were all traditions of this family, who found entertainment in simply being together. These traditions remained an integral part of our family for generations. One of my happiest memories of winter is making snow angels with my mother, who learned this delightful activity from her mother, the youngest child of Alexander's nine children.

Vida describes how her father, Alexander, used to take half a shingle or some pine and create playthings for his children with his pocketknife and a small piece of glass. In addition to the jackstraws mentioned above, he also made useful household tools such as plates, wooden spoons, washboards, and even cupboards. At one time he built a row boat while the children looked on, entranced by what seemed to them a marvelous thing. Vida tells how the lovely little craft was christened with the name *Vida*. "I fairly went dizzy with the honor of it," she admits.

Each winter, the Smith family enjoyed rides in the sleigh. This has been a common activity through the generations, even when I was a child. There are many references in Church history to Joseph and Emma sleigh riding for entertainment, as well as for travel.

And, of course, there were sleigh bells.

Joseph and Emma's granddaughter, Vida, recalls that the wagon was set on runners; hot stones and buffalo robes kept the family warm. Says Vida, "We glided over the snow to the time of the old bells that had rung merry chimes for Father's youthful sleighing parties. Ah, they were deep and clear and full of unusual and jubilant intonations."

In addition to making up funny or wise limericks, the Smith family also enjoyed singing the old church hymns and love songs. Music would have had a special place especially at Christmas, although many of the songs familiar to us today—"White Christmas," "Frosty the Snowman"—had not yet been written. "Silent Night" was written about the time Joseph Smith was thirteen years old. But was it known round the world in his lifetime? While I don't know the answer to that, I do know that music has always retained an important place in every generation of the Smith family. Some members of the Smith family have even written and published their own songs.

Spiritual Treasures

As Latter-day Saints, we celebrate the Savior's birthday on December 25th with the rest of the world. We know, however, through modern revelation that the Savior was actually born on April 6th. Whether we emphasize the tradition of December 25th or the date of

April 6th, we would do well to pause in our commercial enjoyments and to consider the greatest gift of all.

The Lord said to the Prophet Joseph Smith, "Behold I have seen your sacrifices, and will forgive all your sins. . . I am the Lord your God, and through all eternity . . . verily I seal upon you your exaltation" (D&C 132:49-50). Because of the Prophet's obedience to all the Lord gave him to do, he received this promise, which extends to all of us if we will receive the "priceless gifts" restored in this dispensation.

The Prophet Joseph Smith and Emma shared sixteen Christmases and seventeen wedding anniversaries (they were married on January 18, 1827, and he died in June, 1844). Their celebration of the holidays was subject to the circumstances surrounding the work of establishing the Church—with little consideration for their personal wishes.

Regardless of their expectations at Christmas, history records that Joseph and Emma spent their holidays in service to the Church. Their service would ultimately give the world many priceless gifts, including the Book of Mormon, the saving ordinances of the priesthood, and the knowledge that God is our Eternal Father and his Son Jesus Christ is our brother, the Savior of all mankind.

The following chapters chronicle some events surrounding their holidays, and give a list of some of these priceless gifts. This book is written to provide inspirational reading for LDS people, young and old. While care has been taken to relate the historical events as accurately as possible, this book is not intended as an historical resource.

May this simple rehearsal of events surrounding the holidays of Joseph and Emma bless and brighten your life, as it has mine.

1827

The Gift of the Book of Mormon

Joseph and Emma were married without fanfare on January 18, 1827, in South Bainbridge, New York—a few miles form Harmony, Pennsylvania, where Emma's parents, Isaac and Elizabeth Hale, lived. They eloped, and so missed the usual wedding fun.

They went immediately to the home of Joseph's parents, Joseph, Sr., and Lucy Mack Smith. The Smiths lived in a new house located a few miles from Palmyra, New York, and a short distance from the original cabin they had built when they moved from Vermont in 1816. The house was spacious compared to the cabin, but it was still crowded with Joseph's three brothers and two sisters, ranging in age from eight to sixteen. There would have been little privacy for the newlyweds.

On September 22nd this couple shared a most unique experience when they went together, taking a borrowed horse and wagon, to the great hill a few miles away. There, according to previous appointment, Joseph climbed the hill alone and obtained the gold plates from the Angel Moroni. Emma waited for him in the wagon throughout the hours between midnight and dawn. On the way home, they stopped long enough for Joseph to hide the plates in the woods. Later he brought them to the house where they were carefully hidden.

In time word got out that the Smiths supposedly had some "gold plates." While some people ridiculed the very idea that such plates existed, others in the neighborhood had no doubt that the gold plates truly existed. From the time Joseph obtained these plates, ruffians continually harassed the family, trying to obtain this treasure, which was valuable to them only as a means of obtaining money. Joseph understood, as did his family, that the worth of the gold plates was beyond monetary price. Engraved upon them was the priceless gift of the Book of Mormon.

Joseph and his family tried to work, but they were forced to spend a good deal of their time fending off invasions from mobs who were determined to find and take the gold plates. Although he had been given the means for translating the characters on the plates, there was no peace and no safety for them to make the attempt. The situation became so difficult that by December they could no longer remain in Palmyra.

We do not know whether Joseph and Emma spent their first Christmas in Palmyra, enveloped in an atmosphere of persecution, or with her parents, in Harmony, Pennsylvania. There is no mention of the holiday in any contemporary record. We know that sometime in December, Emma's brother Alva went to the Smiths' with his wagon and team. According to Joseph's mother, Lucy Mack Smith, Joseph and Emma loaded up their few possessions—including the gold plates, which they had buried in a barrel of beans—and moved to the home of Emma's parents in Harmony, Pennsylvania. As yet, Joseph had received no direction to organize a "church."

One of the first gifts the couple received was $50 from an old friend and neighbor, Martin Harris. Whether it was in the spirit of Christmas, or simply as a compassionate friend, it helped them make the four-day trip to Harmony, and Joseph and Emma were grateful.

Living in his father-in-law's house, Joseph would have found no sympathy for the knowledge he had received from the Lord, that the religions of the day were "all wrong" and he was to "join none of them." Nevertheless, Joseph was determined to be true to his immediate assignment, which was to care for the safety of the gold plates. He had faith that by the gift and power of God, he would eventually be able to translate the sacred record.

The priceless gift of the Book of Mormon had been delivered into his hands. What price in human effort was yet to be paid, in order to deliver it to the world?

1828

The Gift of Patience

By their first anniversary Joseph and Emma were settled in the Hale hunting cabin, on a thirteen-acre plot of ground they hoped to purchase from Emma's father. The house was old and had been used as a tanning shed and storage place. But they cleaned it out and set up housekeeping. The gold plates lay in a box under their bed.

Emma was expecting their first baby. Since they were dependent on Emma's parents for necessities, it is probable that Emma helped her mother while Joseph found whatever work he could to earn a living.

Between their many outside labors, and Emma's own house-keeping duties, which undoubtedly included candle making, spinning, and weaving and sewing everything they wore, there was little time for them to work on translating the ancient records. But they made an effort, with Emma serving as a scribe.

Things were so peaceful, at that time, they could leave the golden plates lying on the table, wrapped up in a linen table cloth. Despite this, Emma later stated that no one, including herself, was allowed to see the plates. In later years, when asked if she had been vexed at being denied the privilege of seeing the plates, she said she was not. She said she knew Joseph had them, and she knew God had forbidden him to show them to anyone at that time, so she was satisfied. But she did feel their shape and "hefted" them. She said she ran her thumb along the edges, as one thumbs the edges of a book, and they had rustled with a metallic sound. In her old age, she testified that she never doubted they were real and that her husband was exactly what he claimed to be—a prophet of God ("Emma Smith's Last Testimony").

Due to her heavy work load, and the fact that she was expecting a baby, she could find little time or energy to write for Joseph. In April, Martin Harris came to their home to serve as a scribe for Joseph. They made good progress on the translation, completing 116 pages of manuscript by the first part of June.

By then Emma's baby was due shortly. Martin prepared to leave for Palmyra to attend to his own spring work and leave the couple alone while Emma had her baby. He was anxious to show the pages to his wife so as to gain her support of the project and prevailed upon Joseph to let him take the manuscript home. Against all good judgment and the Lord's warnings, Joseph allowed Martin to take the precious pages home.

Within weeks, tragedy struck. Joseph and Emma buried their first child, Alvin, who lived but a short time. Then, before they could recover from that sorrow, they learned that Martin had lost the manuscript upon which he and Joseph had labored so long. It is hard to determine which caused the greater grief—loss of the baby or loss of the manuscript.

As a result of losing the manuscript, the Lord revoked Joseph's privilege to translate, and for a time he feared he had lost his calling. Only after a period of intense sorrow and repentance was he comforted with a revelation telling him he would eventually be able to complete the translation of the record. But the year closed without his being able to move forward in that sacred objective.

Joseph knew the Book of Mormon would be a second witness, with the Bible, of the divinity of Jesus Christ. Knowing the translation of the book had been stopped because he had disregarded the Lord's directions must have made this year's celebration of the Savior's birth a solemn occasion. But through these hard experiences, he gained the priceless gift of patience, which would be his the remainder of his days.

1829

The Gift of Witnesses

In January, Joseph and Emma had, to all outward appearances, laid aside what the Hales considered foolish dreams. If these circumstances pleased Joseph's father-in-law, it must have severely tried the Prophet, who was miserably conscious that his sacred duty was being held in abeyance.

In February, when Joseph's parents visited them, Joseph's mother noticed "a red morocco trunk" on Emma's bureau. Joseph told her it contained the plates and the Urim and Thummim, an instrument provided by the Lord for Joseph to use in translating the record. Joseph mentioned to his mother that if a scribe could be found, the Lord would allow him to translate again (Lucy Mack Smith, *History of Joseph Smith by His Mother,* p. 124).

In April, Oliver Cowdery, a young school teacher, who had lived with Joseph's parents, arrived at their home in Harmony. He offered to serve as scribe. Thus began an association and friendship that would last many years. Through much of that time Oliver would live with them as a member of their family—a dearly loved and trusted friend.

As the translation progressed, Oliver and Joseph shared the incredible experience of receiving the restoration of the Aaronic and Melchizedek priesthoods. These two men were witnesses of the visitations by heavenly beings—John the Baptist and Peter, James, and John, who restored this authority to act in God's name, and taught them to perform the ordinance of baptism. Such an experience makes May 15th a modern-day holy day, and sets it apart for commemoration in the Church throughout the world.

When word got out that these sacred events had occurred, the once peaceful Smith home in Harmony became a center for curiosity seekers and hecklers. Oliver arranged for Joseph and Emma to go to Fayette, New York, to complete the translating at the home of his friend, Peter Whitmer.

After the translation was completed, Oliver, Martin, and one of the Whitmers' sons, David, were shown the gold plates by an angel. They heard the voice of God declare from the heavens that the Book of Mormon had been translated by the gift and power of God.

This gift of witnesses was a special blessing to Joseph, who exclaimed, "Father, Mother, you do not know how happy I am; the Lord has now caused the plates to be shown to three more besides myself . . . It rejoices my soul that I am not any longer to be entirely alone in this world" (Lucy Mack Smith, *History of Joseph Smith by His Mother*, p. 152).

Mother Whitmer, who had opened her home and heart to the Smiths, was given a viewing of the gold plates by an angel (Richard Lloyd Anderson, *Investigating the Witnesses of the Book of Mormon*, p. 31). Though Emma was the prophet's wife, she never saw the plates. But she was witness to the testimony of those who did. We have the priceless gift of Emma's testimony, given not long before she died, in 1879:

> . . . My belief is that the Book of Mormon is of divine authenticity. I have not the slightest doubt of it. . . . Though I was an active participant in the scenes that transpired, and was present during the translation of the plates . . . and had cognizance of things as they transpired, it is marvelous to me, "a marvel and a wonder," as much so as to anyone else. (Jones, *Emma's Glory and Sacrifice: A Testimony*, p. 21)

In addition, eight men saw and handled the gold plates. The testimony of these eleven men stands as a witness for future generations, a solemn declaration of the truth. The plates were real, the translation was real, and they were witnesses to it.

Martin Harris, one of the three witnesses who not only saw the plates but also the angel, provided the needed money for printing the Book of Mormon.

Once again, we have no indication of how Joseph and Emma and their friends celebrated Christmas in 1829. Though the world knew nothing of it, in this fantastic year, a new day was dawning for all mankind. The Book of Mormon translation was complete. The printing process had begun. The Aaronic and Melchizedek Priesthoods were restored. The ordinance of baptism, by the proper authority, had been restored to the earth. The Prophet's father and his brothers, Samuel and Hyrum, along with Joseph, Oliver, and many others, had begun preaching the word, bringing many converts to the waters of baptism.

The priceless gift of witnesses began with the unimpeachable testimony of a few. It has now increased to millions. Of such, the Lord himself might say, as he did to his apostle, Thomas, "Blessed are they that have not seen, yet have believed" (John 20:29).

Restoration of the Aaronic Priesthood

1830

The Gift of the Holy Ghost

The new year brought increasing numbers of people to the knowledge that the Lord had opened the heavens. On April 6, 1830, The Church of Jesus Christ of Latter-day Saints was officially organized in Fayette, New York.

The work of the new year would be to call missionaries, as the Lord had directed them, to eventually carry the news of the Restoration to every nation, kindred, tongue, and people. However, the first missionaries were to go to the Indians, in Western Ohio, which was at that time the farthest western boundary in the United States. Those who were called were enthusiastic about taking the good news to those they referred to as Lamanites, descendants of Lehi, who immigrated to the western hemisphere from Jerusalem about 600 B.C.

The missionaries were zealous to find the Indians and tell them of the Book of Mormon. This book was to be a "voice speaking from the dust" to awaken these descendants of Lehi to the promises made to their ancestors. Its message was to teach them to believe in Jesus Christ and inform them of his visit to their ancestors in ancient times. They were promised that the coming forth of this book to their descendants would be a sign to them that his great restoration work of the latter-days had begun.

The missionaries took leave for the West, and the Prophet and Oliver stayed in New York State to begin the serious work of establishing branches of the Church in that area. One of the first was at Colesville, where in June, their friends Polly and Joseph Knight, Sr., and their entire family, formed the nucleus of stalwart believers. On

June 28th, Emma was baptized, along with about thirteen others. Unfortunately, mobs broke up the meeting before confirmations could be performed. Joseph was forced to take his wife back to Harmony, where he and Oliver were frustrated in being prevented from accomplishing their ministry. Emma, too, was frustrated and wondered when, or if, she would ever be confirmed. She may have even wondered why she was denied certain privileges others were given.

Revelations given to Joseph and Emma, during this time of frustration, defined the role the Lord expected of each of them, and their personal obligation to this, the last dispensation of the gospel.

To Joseph, the calling as a prophet of God was to supercede all other duties. He was not to look for material success in this world, but have faith in the Lord, trusting always that his needs would be supplied (see D&C 24).

To Emma came the admonition not to murmur because of the things she had not seen. Perhaps this revelation laid to rest any feelings Emma might have had about being left out of viewing the plates.

Emma was called an "Elect Lady," and given the assignment to compile a hymn book for the Latter-day Saints. She was told that her specific duty was to be a "comfort to her husband," and she was also warned to "beware of pride," a warning that applied to all members of the Church as well (Doctrine and Covenants section 25).

Early in August, Newell Knight brought his wife, Sally, to Harmony. In a quiet sacrament meeting in the Smith's home, Emma and Sally were confirmed and given the gift of the Holy Ghost.

Before long, excitement spread concerning the new religion. A new wave of persecution brought ugly rumors, which Emma's father believed. This caused him to withdraw his support and protection from them. By the end of August, it was necessary for Joseph and

Emma to leave Harmony. The last thing her father said to them was that he would rather see his daughter go to her grave than go away with Joseph. Sadly, but with faith, Emma said good-bye to her parents—never to see them again on this earth. But for the kindness of the Whitmers, in Fayette, New York, Joseph and Emma would have been homeless.

Christmas 1830, celebrated in the tiny Whitmer cabin, must have been bittersweet. The once close Smith family was scattered throughout various towns in New York State, all having been forced to leave their own homes because of persecution or to pursue their missionary labors. It was a time of loss and a time of gain. The Church was growing. Joseph and Emma had many new friends. Emma, having been baptized in June and confirmed in August, was again looking forward to having another baby.

In December, visitors from the West came to Fayette. Sydney Rigdon and Edward Partridge, who had been introduced to news of the Restoration of the gospel by the missionaries in Ohio, came to see for themselves this modern-day prophet of God. When the two men invited the prophet to return to Ohio with them, Joseph enquired of the Lord what he should do. He received the revelation that he was to "go to the Ohio" (D&C 37:1).

At the end of December 1830 Joseph recorded, "To our great joy and satisfaction, the little flock numbered in all . . . from Colesville to Canandaigua, N.Y. about 70 members" *(History of the Church,* 1:132-33; hereafter referred to as *HC).*

In this year, the priceless gift of the Holy Ghost was received by the Church. The Lord had promised, "And whoso having faith you shall confirm in my church, by the laying on of hands, and I will bestow the gift of the Holy Ghost upon them" (Doctrine and Covenants 33:15).

1831

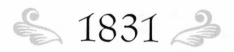

The Gift of Healing

The new members ushered in the new year with a church conference, held on January 2nd, at Fayette, New York, where the Lord said, "Mine eyes are upon you. I am in your midst and ye cannot see me . . . but the day soon cometh that ye shall see me, and know that I am." He further promised, "The veil of darkness [over the earth] shall soon be rent . . ." because of the endowment from on high which would soon be given them (Doctrine and Covenants 38:7-8).

Within a month Joseph and Emma were skimming over the snow in a borrowed sleigh. Ohio was their destination. Emma was pregnant. They were nearly a month on the road, and on the way the sleigh tipped over, but they arrived in Kirtland unharmed. They received a warm welcome from Newell K. Whitney and his wife, Elizabeth, who invited them to stay in their home. Easter, and the anniversary of the founding of the Church, must have elicited special feelings of joy in them all, notwithstanding their homeless circumstances.

Before long Joseph and Emma moved into a log cabin built for them on the Morely Settlement, near Kirtland. There Emma gave birth to twins (April 30), who died after a few short hours. She would record two names, Thaddeus and Louisa, in the family Bible. These names are followed by the names of Joseph and Julia Murdock—twins adopted by Joseph and Emma after their mother died in childbirth.

During this year Joseph traveled to Missouri, where he designated Jackson County as the gathering place for the Church—the site of the future City of Zion. A number of Church members moved there.

That fall, a group of people came to the Smith's home to meet the Prophet. Among them were John Johnson and his wife. Mrs. Johnson had a lame arm, which she could not lift above her head. One of the group asked if supernatural gifts were found in the Church—that is, the power to cure someone such as Mrs. Johnson. Later, Joseph, in a solemn and quiet manner went to her, took her by the hand, and said, "Woman, in the name of the lord Jesus Christ, I command thee to be made whole." The company of people were shocked at his presumption. Mrs. Johnson lifted her healed arm with ease. The next day she was able to do her washing without pain *(HC,* 1:215).

One of the major projects of the Prophet, during 1831, was an intense study and an inspired revision of the Bible. He felt this was prerequisite to all other things yet to be revealed to the Church. He needed peace and quiet for translation, and the John Johnson family invited Joseph's family to move in with them.

The Johnsons had a large farmhouse near Hiram, Ohio. In exchange for room and board, Emma helped Sister Johnson with the household duties. She also spent her days in the role she had so long desired to fill—that of being a mother. The little twins grew and thrived in the peaceful farm atmosphere.

With two sweet babes, a comfortable, peaceful place to live, and surrounded by the friendly Johnson family, this may have been one of the most pleasant holiday seasons Joseph and Emma had spent since they were married. All during December, Joseph concentrated on translating the Bible and preaching the gospel. He also hoped to allay people's fears, which had been aroused by the proliferation of anti-Mormon publications.

As the year came to a close, Joseph came to understand that, according to the mind and will of the Lord, the time had come for the gospel to be proclaimed, in power and demonstration, to the world (see *HC,* 1:239). Not only would God give the Church the priesthood, the power to heal the body, but eventually, through the restoration of all things, he will one day bestow the priceless gift of eternal healing—that is, the resurrection—for all mankind.

1832

The Gift of Testimony

With the new year there came sacred visions for the Prophet and his associates. In the upper chamber of old Father Johnson's home, a group of the brethren gathered. There Joseph and Sidney received a revelation that would dispel the ignorance of centuries and reveal the plan of God concerning the purpose and destiny of mankind.

Surrounded by the glory of the vision, they declared, "The Lord touched the eyes of our understandings. . . . [And] we beheld the glory of the Son, on the right hand of the Father." This vision allowed them to testify boldly, "And now, after the many testimonies which have been given of him, this is the testimony, last of all, which we give of him; that he lives! For we saw him, even on the right hand of God; and we heard the voice bearing record that he is the only Begotten of the Father. . . ." (Doctrine and Covenants 76:19-23).

This testimony was followed within a few short weeks by a time of bitter persecution and tragic loss. In March, a mob broke into the Johnson's house and dragged the Prophet out. Joseph was stripped and beaten, and his body was covered with tar. When the mob had finished, Joseph was left lying on the frozen ground, unconscious. Emma, who was expecting another child, was frantic as she waited helplessly, fearing the worst. When Joseph came to himself, he made his way to the house, calling for a blanket to cover his nakedness. Emma, seeing the tar on his body, thought it was blood and fainted. She and the Johnsons worked all night to remove the tar. The next morning Joseph preached a sermon on brotherly love.

A few days later, their eleven-month-old baby, little Joseph Murdock, died from pneumonia, caused by his exposure to the cold night air when the mob invaded their home. In view of the mob spirit in the neighborhood, Joseph left for Missouri with Newell K. Whitney; Emma went back to Kirtland with little Julia. Left without house or home and suffering from the nausea of early pregnancy, Emma was forced to board first one place and then another, never sure where she would be staying or for how long. Joseph returned months later, noting that he found Emma "most disconsolate." An apartment was prepared above the Whitney Store, but Joseph could not stay with her. He went to Boston, Albany, and New York City, preaching the gospel and buying paper for the printing of the revelations.

Emma's fears must have been great after losing three infants, and when Joseph wrote to her from New York, he expressed his understanding of her "peculiar fears." (He knew, as others did not, that she was once again expecting a child.) By letter he declared himself her "one true and devoted friend on earth." What longing she must have had for that friend to be beside her day by day (Joseph to Emma, October 1832; letter in author's possession).

For Christmas Joseph was home in Kirtland. He and Emma settled in a comfortable three-room apartment above the Whitney Store in Kirtland, Ohio. Their newly born son, Joseph Smith III, was now six weeks old, and he—along with nineteenth-month-old Julia—filled Emma's days with happy mothering. By this time, Joseph's parents, brothers, and sisters had gathered in Kirtland. Missionary work was spreading throughout the United States and Canada at a rapid rate. In Missouri, Joseph had dedicated the sight for a future temple, and the Saints looked forward to building Zion in that land.

During this season the brethren received instruction at the School of the Prophets. This school was first organized in March 1832, and met in Joseph and Emma's apartment. Many wonderful revelations were received there. In one such revelation, the Lord called the Saints "my friends" (Doctrine and Covenants 84:77).

Since the entire family was in close proximity, it is possible they gathered for parties and socials to celebrate the holidays. But the records we have are silent concerning their personal doings. We do not even know for sure where Joseph was when, on Christmas Day, he received the famous prophecy on war—accurately predicting, thirty years before the fact, the terrible Civil War between the northern and southern states—as well as future world wars that would involve all nations.

Ironically, on Christmas Eve, a thousand miles away, unknown to the Prophet, some of the Saints in Jackson County were driven into the winter night by ruthless mobs who hated and feared the Latter-day Saints because of their desire to build Zion in Jackson County.

Around this same time, an article published by Joseph in the church newspaper admonished the Saints to be humble, meek, and submissive in tribulation. He said that those who would not bear persecution were not worthy to be called Saints. In a revelation given on December 27th, the Lord once again called the Saints "my friends," and added, "Draw near unto me and I will draw near unto you" (Doctrine and Covenants 88:62, 63).

Never had a people received greater evidence that they had been chosen and that they had received truth upon which they could build Zion in the latter days.

In this precarious world, how desperately they would need the priceless gift of faith.

Emma's Hymns

1833

The Gift of Hope

At the beginning of 1833, the Prophet Joseph recorded that he had "many glorious seasons of refreshing. The gifts which follow them that believe and obey the Gospel, as tokens that the Lord is ever the same in His dealings with the humble lovers and followers of truth, began to be poured out among us, as in ancient days. . . ." *(HC,* 1:322).

Joseph began the new year winding up the work he had spent so much time on during the previous year. He observed, "I completed the translation and review of the New Testament, on the 2ⁿᵈ of February, 1833 and sealed it up. . . ." (ibid., p. 324).

Now the hopes of the Saints were directed toward establishing Zion, this year, in Jackson County, Missouri.

On April 6ᵗʰ, in the land of Zion (Jackson County), at the ferry on the Big Blue River, about eighty Church members celebrated the anniversary of the birthday of the Church, and the birth of Jesus Christ. The following was recorded in *The History of the Church*:

> The day was spent in a very agreeable manner, in giving and receiving knowledge which appertained to this last kingdom—it being just 1800 years since the Savior laid down His life that men might have everlasting life, and only three years since the Church had come out of the wilderness, preparatory for the last dispensation. The Saints had great reason to rejoice: they thought upon the time when this world came into existence, and the morning stars sang together, and all the sons of God shouted for joy; they thought of the time when Israel ate the "Passover," as

wailing came up for the loss of the firstborn of Egypt; they felt
like the shepherds who watched their flocks by night, when the
angelic choir sweetly sang the electrifying strain, "Peace on earth,
good will to man;" and the solemnities of eternity rested upon
them. (*HC*,1:337)

Citizens in Jackson County, who were not of the faith, considered
the singing of Christmas carols, in April, as "a strange thing." Their
suspicions of the Saints increased.

Meanwhile, back in Kirtland, preparations were underway to
build a temple. On June 5th Hyrum Smith and Reynolds Cahoon
began digging the trench for the walls of the Lord's House. George A.
Smith hauled the first load of stone for the temple, where the Saints
hoped to receive further light and knowledge from the Lord.

About a week before Christmas, Joseph dedicated a printing office
situated by the temple site in Kirtland. There he hoped to fulfill the
commandment to send the scriptures to the world.

Among the many revelations given during 1833, was the Word of
Wisdom, a law simple in its basic principles of healthful living, yet
cutting across every social and cultural barrier, which would, in time,
test the faith of all Saints, rich and poor, old and young. A hundred
years after it was given, medical evidence would support its valid
premise: the healthfulness of abstaining from tobacco, liquor, and hot
drinks (i.e., coffee and tea), and of eating meat in moderation. The
Word of Wisdom would become one of the prerequisites, along with
moral living, for obtaining a recommend to enter into the temple.

Expanding church organization called for a patriarch to the
Church. The prophet's father, Joseph Smith, Sr., was called to fill this
office. He was ordained on December 18th in the new printing office
the same day it was dedicated. The Prophet's family rejoiced at the
evidence that God was directing the work of establishing his Church
on the earth.

As the walls of the temple were rising, every inch of space in Joseph and Emma's apartment above the store was filled with people sleeping at night, and eating and studying in the daytime. With Don Carlos, Joseph's youngest brother, and Oliver Cowdery also staying with them that Christmas, it soon became evident that Joseph and Emma needed a bigger house in which to live. Perhaps Emma hoped that this would happen in the new year to come.

The year 1833 closed with tragic news from Missouri, where the Latter-day Saints had been under siege by angry mobs. In November, hundreds of men, women, and children lined the shores of the Missouri River—driven from their homes into the winter wilderness. On Christmas Eve, the Jackson County mobs struck against four families, who had, because of age and infirmities, been unable to leave the area with the others who had fled. These elderly people, veterans of the American Revolution, humble, quiet souls who had never done anyone harm, were "driven from their homes . . . [while] the mob . . . tore down their chimneys, broke in their doors and windows, and hurled large stones into their houses" (*HC,* 1:69).

However, not all nonmembers in Jackson County approved of this behavior, and later in the month the perpetrator of the cruel deeds was arrested for his actions.

Parley P. Pratt, who was with the outcast Saints camped outside the Jackson County line, recorded a spectacular sight in the heavens:

> [About two o'clock in the morning] we were called up by the cry of signs in the heavens. . . . To our great astonishment all the firmament seemed enveloped in splendid fireworks, as if every star in the broad expanse had been hurled from its course. . . Thousands of bright meteors were shooting through space in every direction, with long trains of light following in their course. This lasted for several hours, and was only closed by the dawn of the rising sun. Every heart was filled with joy at this majestic display of signs and wonders. (*Autobiography of Parley P. Pratt,* p. 103)

This display was seen throughout the country, and Joseph, who saw it in Kirtland, was led to exclaim, "How marvelous are Thy works, O Lord! I thank Thee for Thy mercy unto Thy servant: save me in Thy kingdom for Christ's sake. Amen" *(HC,* 1:439).

The Saints who saw the spectacular display viewed it as a heavenly manifestation and received the priceless gift of hope.

1834

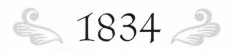

The Gift of Discernment

The new year dawned on a massive relief effort for the Church members who had been driven from their homes in Missouri. The Prophet was away from home most of that year, either gathering up men or making the march with them in what became known as Zion's Camp.

In Kirtland, Emma continued to board Oliver Cowdery, and others, in her scanty space, while she tended her two small children. The family had little time together and no privacy. While personal information about the family is limited, I have copies of two letters written to Emma from the "Camp of Israel" during the long trek to Missouri. Certainly Joseph's absence from home was a hardship for her and the children—perhaps the best gift of the holidays was simply a letter from Joseph.

Each of these letters is filled with details of the people and places of his journey. Undoubtedly Emma found these details interesting; however, missing her husband as she did, she would probably have read and reread Joseph's words of a more personal nature, such as the following: "I sit down in my tent to write a few lines to you to let you know that you are on my mind and that I am sensible of the duties of a husband and father and that I am well and I pray God to let his blessings rest upon you and the children and all that are around you until I return to your society. . . . O may the blessings of God rest upon you is the prayer of your husband until death . . ." (Joseph to Emma, 18 May 1834).

He also expressed his appreciation for her many letters, which he said gave him "satisfaction and comfort and I hope you will continue to communicate to me by your own hand for this is a consolation to me to converse with you in this way in my lonely moments which is not easily described" (ibid.).

His second letter, written after much travel over plains and rivers, tells that he had been quite well on the journey, but had suffered blistered feet, which had healed. He described "gazing upon a country the fertility, the splendor, and the goodness so indescribable, all serve to pass away time unnoticed, and in short, were it not at every now and then our thoughts linger with inexpressible anxiety for our wives and our children our kindred according to the flesh that are entwined around our hearts; and also our brethren and friends; our whole journey would be as a dream, and this would be the happiest period of all our lives" (Joseph to Emma, 4 June 1834).

His closing in this letter is especially poignant, in light of the fact that they were on their way to Missouri, not knowing what battles might lie ahead. "Tell Father Smith and all the family, and brother Oliver to be comforted and look forward to the day when the trials and tribulations of that life will be at an end, and we all enjoy the fruits of our labour if we hold out faithful to the end, which I pray may be the happy lot of us all." He signed this letter, "From yours in the bonds of affliction" (ibid.).

Unfortunately, any letters Emma may have written to Joseph during this separation were not preserved.

Zion's Camp was not successful in returning the Missouri Saints to their lands in Jackson County. Nevertheless, much good was accomplished in bringing aid and comfort to the scattered Saints who had settled in Clay County. The experience also helped Joseph to identify the men who could be trusted, as well as those who could not—thus bestowing on him the gift of discernment.

After an absence of nearly four months, Joseph's homecoming to Kirtland must have been a day of great rejoicing for his family. But whatever household tasks Emma may have saved up for him would have to wait. Within three days of his return, the pace of Church business, the need to settle disputes among some of the brethren, and harassment from false charges from former brethren, all demanded his attention.

Amidst these accusations, Joseph stood his ground with faith, writing to his brethren in Missouri, saying, "I have succeeded in putting all gainsayers and enemies to flight, unto the present time; and notwithstanding the adversary laid a plan, which was more subtle than all others. . . . I now swim in good, clean water, with my head out" (HC, 2:144).

The business of the year consisted of endless organizational meetings as well as a continued effort to build the temple. Joseph, dressed in a tow-frock (a baggy sort of overall generally worn by the workmen), labored with the others in the quarry. At the same time period, he was also preparing to resume the School of the Prophets. In November he observed, "No month ever found me more busily engaged . . . but as my life consisted of activity and unyielding exertions, I made this my rule: When the Lord commands, do it" (HC, 2:170).

This school, which was also called the school of the elders was at this time presided over by Parley P. Pratt and was very well attended. The purpose of this schooling was to prepare the brethren who were to be sent out into the world to preach the gospel, to qualify themselves "as messengers of Jesus Christ, to be ready to do His will in carrying glad tidings to all that would open their eyes, ears and hearts" (HC, 2:176).

Through the hardships of the year, Joseph had attuned his heart to listen to the promptings that came to him from the Lord. He was stern in his admonition that the Saints become more united and strove to instruct them in their own efforts to be in tune with the Lord's will.

On December 9th, Emma and Joseph received their patriarchal blessings. Emma's blessing reflects the Lord's awareness of her faith, sacrifices, and sorrows. She was reassured that the death of her babies was not her fault, and she was promised she would yet have more children.

Joseph's blessing confirmed his prophetic calling, making many promises of an eternal nature for both him and his posterity.

The School of the Prophets met regularly during the winter of 1834. In the Prophet's history for December, he says, "The classes, being mostly Elders, gave the most studious attention to the all-important object of qualifying themselves as messengers of Jesus Christ—to be ready to do His will in carrying glad tidings to all that would open their eyes, ears and hearts" *(HC,* 2:176).

There is no mention of Christmas in Joseph's history record for that year, but it appears that at least Joseph was at home for the holidays.

1835

The Gift of Knowledge

The year of 1835 brought more schooling for the elders of the Church, more priesthood organization, and many revelations. For Joseph, it brought much travel back and forth between Kirtland and Missouri.

Within this year the Church became organized with a First Presidency, Twelve Apostles, and priesthood quorums.

For Emma, it meant weeks and months of coping with her little children by herself, coping with Joseph's business affairs in his absence, and coping with a growing animosity from enemies who published lies and harassed her husband with lawsuits.

But it also contained time for sleighing for pleasure, visiting friends in surrounding areas, and attending family gatherings and weddings.

During the fall there was a serious conflict between Joseph and his brother William, who became contentious when Joseph corrected him. This resulted in hurt feelings all around, and made it difficult for Joseph in his effort to prepare the Saints for the dedication of the Kirtland Temple. Joseph Smith, Sr., and his wife, Lucy, had been living with William and were uncomfortable with the discord between their sons. For this reason, Joseph invited his parents and youngest sister, Lucy, to move in with his family.

Early in December there was an uncommonly heavy snowstorm, with sufficient snow for sleighing. Joseph took his wife and children to Painesville in the sleigh. They enjoyed dinner with friends, then "had a fine ride. The sleighing was good and weather pleasant."

On his birthday, December 23rd, Joseph remained "at home studying the Greek language." The same day he exhibited the Egyptian artifacts to visitors. Joseph's language study during this year had also included Hebrew and other languages as well.

One of the activities of the winter was debating, but Joseph admonished the Saints to "handle sacred things very sacredly and with due deference to the opinions of others and with an eye single to the glory of God." Undoubtedly, his urgency on this subject was fostered by the falling out with his brother, William (Faulring, *Diaries and Journals of Joseph Smith*, p. 66).

That Christmas Joseph wrote, "Enjoyed myself with my family, it being Christmas day, the only time I have had this privilege so satisfactorily for a long time" *(HC,* 2:345).

With the reprinting of the Book of Mormon, the preparation of the revelations for printing, and the excitement at receiving the Book of Abraham, the priceless gift of knowledge was greatly appreciated by the Saints.

1836

The Gift of Humility

The temple was nearing completion as the year 1836 began. On New Year's Day, Joseph wrote:

> This being the beginning of a new year, my heart is filled with gratitude to God that He has preserved my life, and the lives of my family, while another year has passed away. We have been sustained and upheld in the midst of a wicked and perverse generation, although exposed to all the afflictions, temptations, and misery that are incident to human life; for this I feel to humble myself in dust and ashes, as it were, before the Lord. (*HC*, 2:428)

Reflecting upon the events of the past year, the Prophet found much to be elated about. However, he was also troubled. He recorded:

> My heart is pained within me, because of the difficulty that exists in my father's family. The devil has made a violent attack on my brother William and [brother-in-law] Calvin Stoddard, and the powers of darkness seem to lower over their minds, and not only theirs, but they also cast a gloomy shade over the minds of my brethren and sisters, which prevents them from seeing things as they really are; and the powers of earth and hell seem combined to overthrow us and the Church, by causing a division in the family. . . . (*HC*, 2:352)

Furthermore, the trouble had spread to the priesthood quorums, with "the adversary bringing into requisition all his subtlety to prevent the Saints from being endowed . . ."(ibid.).

The Lord had promised that when the temple was completed they would receive an endowment from on high. In preparation for this wonderful blessing, it was essential that the Saints be reconciled with one another and it would begin with the Smith family.

On New Year's Day Father Smith called his family together, and with great urgency and tenderness, he brought reconciliation between Joseph and William. The rest of the family was then called to join in, with all covenanting to henceforth give one another support and love rather than quarreling. Thereafter, the spirit of reconciliation spread abroad in the Church as well, as all prepared to be found worthy to dedicate the House of the Lord.

In February, Emma's collection of sacred hymns, and the Doctrine and Covenants, came off the press. Previously, the Missouri persecutions had delayed the printing of these books; now these publications were greeted with great enthusiasm.

The Kirtland Temple was dedicated March 27th, with over 930 people in attendance. Concluding his prayer, the Prophet asked the Lord to hear their petitions and "accept the dedication of this house . . . the work of our hands, which we have built unto they name." As on the day of Pentecost, the Holy Spirit was manifest in tongues of fire, and heavenly manifestations occurred at the dedication. People outside the temple thought the temple was on fire *(HC,* 2:352).

The Savior, Moses, Elias, and Elijah appeared to Joseph and Oliver in the Kirtland Temple, and at last, all the keys of the dispensation of the fullness of times were restored.

Sometime before 1836, Joseph and Emma moved their family into a larger house not far from the Chagrin River. Emma was expecting another baby, and with all the boarders (there were from three to five in residence constantly), they had outgrown the little apartment above the store. Frederick was born June 20th.

The Saints began to establish new communities in the northern part of Missouri, and the brethren extended their missionary efforts. Financial distress drove Joseph to Salem, New York, in a foolish hope of finding money to defray his debts. Instead, he found records of his ancestors, and more members joined the Church as a result of the elders' extensive preaching throughout the country. Joseph and his traveling companions returned home spiritually uplifted, but as beset with financial woes as ever. In answer to his prayers, he received a promise from the Lord that all their needs would be met—in due time. The lesson that even prophets must endure hardship was humbling to all.

At Christmas time, all the family members were back in Kirtland from their missions. Times were hard financially, but the Smith family was not daunted by poverty. Brothers, sisters, parents, uncles, aunts and cousins were united in the cause of the gospel.

Translation of the Bible

1837

The Gift of Faith

The year of 1837 brought a renewed effort to pull out of financial distress. The Kirtland Safety Society, a proposed banking system, was organized with high hopes.

In June, missionaries left to open a mission in England. Their faith, as they left under such conditions of poverty and sickness, is a priceless gift to us.

In spite of the Prophet's advice to be careful in all their dealings, speculation grasped the minds of many Latter-day Saints as part of the westward expansionism going on all over the country. Many of the Saints overextended themselves in the expectation of making a great deal of money by buying on credit and selling on credit. Eliza R. Snow wrote, "As the Saints drank in the love and spirit of the world, the Spirit of the Lord withdrew from their hearts, and they were filled with pride and hatred toward those who maintained their integrity" (Eliza R. Snow letters, LDS Archives). A spirit of greed seemed to affect even some of the most trusted men of the Church.

By the end of the year, the entire country was in the grasp of a depression and the Safety Society had failed (along with many other banks throughout the land). In Kirtland, apostasy was rampant. Nearly half of the twelve apostles ". . . linked themselves together in an opposing party—pretending that they constituted the church, and claimed that the Temple belonged to them, and even attempted to hold it" (*HC*, 2:488 ftnt.). A new home had been under construction for Joseph and Emma, but when Kirtland money was no longer accepted, all construction in the city stopped.

Joseph was frequently away from home—either in Missouri or the East. Emma had to cope with apostates who tried to take all Joseph had in the way of possessions. In great distraction over this, she wrote in a letter to Joseph: "I have been so treated that I have come to the determination not to let any man or woman have anything whatever without being well assured that it goes to your own advantage, but it is impossible for me to do anything as long as everybody has so much better right to all that is called yours than I have" (Emma to Joseph, May 3, 1837).

That fall a desolating tragedy occurred in the family when Hyrum's wife, Jerusha, died in childbirth, leaving him with a large family. Jerusha's last words to her children were simply that she had to go and was leaving them to be cared for by their father. At the time she died, Hyrum was in Missouri on church business. When he returned, the Prophet told him to marry Mary Fielding, who was highly esteemed by the Smith family, and was already taking care of Hyrum's motherless children.

This was a time of great tribulation within the Church. Apostates raged in Kirtland. When Brigham Young stood up to them, he was forced to leave Kirtland for his own safety. He left on December 22nd after apostates threatened to kill him because he proclaimed publicly and privately that he knew "by the power of the Holy Ghost that Joseph was a Prophet of the Most High God" *(HC,* 2:528).

Young Joseph was five years old at the time and later recalled that he had been promised a little wagon, probably for Christmas. It was being built by a wagon-maker not far from their home. Impatient to possess the wagon, he slipped away from home one day and peeked in through the crack in the siding of the shop. He said, "I saw the wagon nicely painted red and awaiting the finishing touches before it was to be delivered . . . Strange to say I have no recollection of ever having used it" *(Memoirs of Joseph Smith III,* p. 2). It is quite likely that the little wagon was never purchased, as money became nonexistent with the financial crash that occurred that winter.

Joseph III also remembers visiting the Church farm with his father when a goose was caught and killed, which may have been for their holiday dinner.

Although, in Kirtland, the year closed on scenes of horrible mob violence, the faithful efforts of the missionaries in England were bearing fruit. On Christmas Day, the first public conference of the LDS church ever held in England was attended by about three hundred Saints.

The example of Brigham Young, and others who supported the prophet and the Church in this time of severe trial, is a priceless gift of faith.

1838

The Gift of Cheerfulness in Tribulation

Early in January, Joseph realized his life was in danger and that he must leave Kirtland. He had not yet completed his preparations to leave, when, according to his mother, "He was warned by the Spirit to make his escape, with his family, as speedily as possible" (Lucy Mack Smith, *History of Joseph Smith By His Mother,* p. 248). Joseph arose from his bed and notified Sydney Rigdon. The two men left that very night.

Thus, while expecting another baby, Emma found it necessary to gather up her belongings for yet another journey. Joseph's youngest brother, Don Carlos Smith, helped Emma and the children—Julia (6), Joseph (5), and Freddie (1)—travel to a neighboring town, where she met Joseph.

The Smiths and the Rigdons traveled together across Ohio, Indiana, Illinois, Iowa, and Missouri—to Far West, a new town that was being built by the Saints. They met Brigham Young and his family at Terre Haute, Indiana, and continued west together, crossing the treacherous Mississippi on the ice. Brigham Young would later remark that he learned how to lead an exodus, from the master leader, Joseph Smith, on this trip.

The Prophet and his family arrived in Far West in March. Joseph was immediately engaged in Church duties and decisions concerning the apostasy of some of their closest friends, including Oliver Cowdery and David Whitmer. He also went to survey a new town, Adam-ondi-Ahman, about twenty-five miles to the north, in Clay County. Joseph returned to Far West in time to be with Emma when she gave birth to my great-grandfather, Alexander Hale Smith, on June 2nd.

On July 4ᵗʰ they celebrated Independence Day, with a parade, speeches, and raising of the flag. When lightning struck the flagpole, Joseph took it as a bad sign. Several children standing nearby, later recalled this event. One child, Oliver DeMille, remembered, "I heard the prophet say, 'Just as that has been stricken down, our liberty shall be taken from us, every vestige'" (Jones, *Emma's Glory and Sacrifice,* p. 81).

Emma turned 33 on July 10ᵗʰ. She was a busy mother with four little ones to tend.

Joseph was working hard at this time trying to set up communities for the Saints. Temple sites were dedicated at both Far West and Adam-ondi-Ahman.

Missouri's politicians watched with growing concern as large numbers of refugees poured in from Kirtland, as well as converts from Canada, the southern states, and England. Their friendliness with the Indians and their acceptance of Blacks roused anger against the Mormons. By the end of October, the governor, Lilburn Boggs, acting on rumors and goaded by enemies of the Church, issued an order that all Mormons must leave Missouri or be exterminated. Shocked at the unconstitutional order, the Saints tried to seek protection in the courts, but to no avail. When they resorted to arming themselves to fight, if necessary, for their homes and property, they suddenly became "the enemy." War was imminent.

During these difficult days, the Saints often struggled for the bare necessities. Joseph III recalled that, as a young boy, food was scarce. "One day all we had to eat for dinner was corn bread made from corn meal with only the addition of salt and water, and seasoned as we ate with New Orleans molasses." An elder in the Church was visiting for dinner, and in spite of the circumstances, the conversation that took place was cheerful. The elder remarked on Emma's corn bread: "Why, with a chunk of corn bread like that in my hand I could go out of doors and stand at the corner of the house in the northwest wind and eat myself into a sweat!" (*Memoirs of Joseph III,* p. 3).

There would have been no Christmas celebration in the family that year—only anxiety, loneliness, and fear. It would be a lonely Christmas for Emma and her little family. She visited Joseph in Liberty Jail at least three times. One of her visits was on December 8th, another, on the 20th. At that time affidavits were prepared showing that apostates had broken into her home, taking whatever they pleased, including all her bedding. This was a terrible hardship, not only for Emma and the children, but for Joseph as well. When he asked Emma to bring him some blankets, she wept because all she had was one quilt and one blanket. Sending them would leave her children with nothing to protect them from the cold winter nights. The Butlers, converts to the Church, heard of the situation and provided Emma and the children with blankets. This occurred in late December (William G. Hartley, *My Best for the Kingdom*, p. 86).

Plans were under way for Emma to take the children and leave Missouri. She was reluctant to go, but the sheriff informed her that if she left Missouri, her husband and the others would more than likely be released. In a letter to Joseph, she said:

> Was it not for conscious innocence and the direct interposition of divine mercy, I am very sure I never should have been able to have endured the scenes of suffering that I have passed through . . . but I still live and am yet willing to suffer more if it is the will of kind heaven that I should for your sake. (Emma to Joseph, 7 March 1839, Letter in RLDS Archives)

While in jail at Liberty, Missouri, Joseph wrote, "Dearly beloved brethren, let us cheerfully do all things that lie in our power; and then may we stand still, with the utmost assurance, to see the salvation of God, and for his arm to be revealed" (Doctrine and Covenants 123:17).

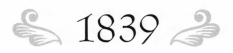

1839

The Gift of Compassion

Emma set out across the muddy prairie in a wagon driven by Stephen Markham, with Julia, young Joseph, Freddie, and Alexander, a babe in arms. After nine days, they arrived at the Mississippi River. On February 15th, Emma and the children crossed the frozen river on foot because it was not safe to ride in the wagon.

Kindly folks took them in, once they reached Quincy, Illinois. A home was found, on a farm owned by the Cleveland family near Quincy. There the refugees crowded in together, giving one another encouragement and aid.

According to letters written by Don Carlos, to Joseph and Hyrum, we know that this faithful younger brother was looking after the needs of their wives and the children, and Mother and Father Smith *(HC, 3:272-74)*.

On April 22nd, a ragged, dirty, emaciated Joseph approached the house where his family waited. Emma, who had been warned of his coming, waited for him at the gate. He had been allowed to escape from Missouri by sympathetic guards who realized he would never get a fair trial. This reunion was the occasion for a joyous celebration for his family and the Church.

In May, Joseph settled his family in the swampy town of Commerce (later known as Nauvoo), Illinois. They made their home in a two-story log cabin on the banks of the Mississippi. As the Saints settled in the swampy country, sickness and poverty plagued them.

At the end of October, Sidney Rigdon, Joseph, and Elias Higbee, left for Washington, D.C., to seek federal action against the state of Missouri for the unconstitutional treatment it had heaped upon certain citizens of the United States.

At Christmas, Joseph was still in Washington, D.C. Emma found herself destitute of almost every necessity of life. The situation must have been made even more difficult for her since she was expecting another baby. We read in the *History of the Church* that "the high council at Nauvoo voted . . . [that] Bishop Knight provide for the families of Joseph Smith Jun., Sidney Rigdon . . . during their absence at Washington" (*HC,* 4:46). In fact, hunger stalked every family. Few Saints had even the basic necessities. Hyrum wrote to Joseph telling him, "Bishop Knight desires me to inform you, that Brothers Granger and Haws have driven into Commerce a large number of hogs. They are now engaged in slaughtering them" *(HC,* 4:52).

Young Joseph remembered that during his father's absence, his mother, Emma, filled her house and yard with the sick, "who were brought to her from near and far, giving them shelter, treatment and nursing care" (Joseph III, *Memoirs,* p. 6b).

Perhaps the suffering that Emma endured during her winter treks across the Missouri wilderness prepared her tender heart for the great service she was to render her fellow man. Ever after she would welcome the poor, needy, and homeless—nursing the sick and giving liberally of whatever she had to share. She had learned, from experience after experience, what it was like to be a refugee. The gift of compassion was hers. Her compassionate example is her gift to us.

1840

The Gift of Forgiveness

The year of 1840 is summed up in two letters. Joseph wrote to Emma two days after their thirteenth wedding anniversary: "I am filled with constant anxiety and shall be until I git home. I pray god to spare you all until I git home my dear Emma, my heart is entwined around you and those little ones." In their thirteen years of marriage, they had endured almost constant persecution, deprivation, poverty, and separation. Ironically, much of their suffering was caused by the treachery of those they had considered to be their friends (Joseph to Emma, January 20, 1840; letter in author's possession).

Joseph came home from Washington, D.C., in March. He would be gone again most of the year, although he did manage to be at her side when Emma gave birth, on June 13th, to another son. They named the baby Don Carlos, after Joseph's brother, whom they both adored.

By the end of the year, the town they were building had a new name: Nauvoo, meaning "beautiful resting place." At last, surrounded by faithful friends and protected by a city charter that provided for a local court system, Joseph was able to pick up the threads of his prophetic calling. After all they had endured, it is doubtful Emma minded that Joseph's business was conducted, for the most part, in her kitchen.

Joseph's father died in September. The whole Church grieved at the death of their beloved patriarch, feeling that his life had been shortened by the persecutions in Missouri.

Many important things happened in 1840, but none more important than Joseph's effort to reconcile with former associates.

Some had been estranged due to error or misunderstanding, others through outright wicked behavior. Now, in more secure circumstances, the Prophet had time to reflect on the personal tragedies of friends who had not withstood the trials of Kirtland and Missouri. He wrote many letters inviting them to repent and come to Nauvoo.

William W. Phelps received one of these letters. The loss of his friendship had been heartbreaking to Joseph and Emma. In the early days of the Church, he had often stayed in their home and had helped edit and print the revelations, the hymnal, and the first Church newspaper, *The Evening and Morning Star.* Then, in 1833, the Phelps' house in Independence was razed and the press destroyed. In the wake of awful persecution, Phelps had had a serious misunderstanding with the Church leaders and was excommunicated. Joseph had been especially hurt when Phelps testified against him at the hearing at Richmond.

In response to Joseph's letter, Phelps wrote, "I have seen the folly of my way, and I tremble at the gulf I have passed . . . I will repent and live, and ask my old friends to forgive me" *(HC,* 4:141).

Joseph replied:

> When we read your letter, truly our hearts melted. . . . It is true we have suffered much in consequence of your behavior. The cup of gall, already full enough . . . was indeed filled to over-flowing, when you turned against us. . . . However, the cup has been drunk. The will of the Father has been done, and we are yet alive, for which we thank the Lord. . . . Believing your confession to be real and your repentance genuine, I shall be happy once again to give you the right hand of fellowship and rejoice over the returning prodigal. . . . Come, dear brother, since the war is past. For friends at first are friends at last. (*HC,* 4:163-64)

Others also responded and were reconciled, showing a profound example of the Prophet's forgiving nature. The priceless gift of forgiveness, as evidenced by the Prophet Joseph Smith, is ever and always the essence of the Savior's mission.

You Shall be a Comfort

1841

The Gift of Baptism for the Dead

In January 1841, Nauvoo was staffing its offices for mayor and city council, and was rapidly exercising its rights as a newly incorporated city in Illinois. A unique canal system was being dug that would drain the swamps and make the area more healthy. During this year many converts arrived from England, bringing their old world skills that would be reflected in the architecture and culture of the community. Nauvoo's rapid development was astonishing the entire country.

During this time, spiritual blessings flowed abundantly to the Church. One of the most comforting blessings to come during this time was the doctrine of baptism for the dead, which Joseph had introduced while preaching a funeral sermon in 1840. On December 15, 1840, Joseph had written to the members of the Twelve who were in England to explain what was happening:

> I presume the doctrine of "Baptism for the dead" has ere this reached your ears, and may have raised some inquiries in your mind respecting the same. I cannot in this letter give you all the information you may desire on the subject, but aside from my knowledge independent of the Bible, I would say, that this was certainly practiced by the ancient Churches and St. Paul endeavors to prove the doctrine of the resurrection from the same, and says "else what shall they do who are baptized for the dead" etc., etc. I first mentioned the doctrine in public while preaching the funeral sermon of Bro. Brunson, and have since then given general instructions to the Church on the subject. The saints have the privilege of being baptized for those of their relatives who are dead, who they feel to believe would have embraced the gospel if they had been privileged with hearing it . . . and who have received the gospel in the spirit through the instrumentality of

those who may have been commissioned to preach to them. . . .
[in the spirit world]. (Joseph Smith to Twelve; see Jessee, *The
Personal Writings of Joseph Smith*, p. 486)

Joseph went on to add, ". . . You will undoubtedly see its consis-
tency, and reasonableness, and [it] presents the gospel of Christ in
probably a more enlarged scale than some have viewed it" (ibid.).

After the doctrine was announced to the Saints in Nauvoo, they
joyfully began to participate in vicarious baptism for their dead loved
ones. The first baptisms for the dead were performed in the
Mississippi River. However, in view of the Lord's command that
the temple was the more suitable place for this work, the Saints
redoubled their efforts to build that sacred building. Even before the
entire temple could be constructed, a temporary baptismal font
was built.

This interesting description of the first baptismal font built for
this purpose is recorded in the *History of the Church:*

> The baptismal font is situated in the center of the basement
> room, under the main hall of the Temple; it is constructed of
> pine timber, and put together of staves tongued and grooved,
> oval shaped, sixteen feet long east and west, and twelve feet wide,
> seven feet high from the foundation, the basin four feet deep, the
> moulding of the cap and base are formed of beautiful carved
> work in antique style. The sides are finished with panel work. A
> flight of stairs in the north and south sides lead up and down
> into the basin, guarded by side railing.
>
> The font stands upon twelve oxen, four on each side, and
> two on each end, their heads, shoulders, and four legs projecting
> out from under the font; they are carved out of pine plank, glued
> together, and copied after the most beautiful five-year old steer
> that could be found in the country. . .The oxen and ornamental
> mouldings of the font were carved by Elder Elijah Fordham . . .
> and occupied eight months of time. The font was enclosed by a
> temporary frame building sided up with split oak clapboards,
> with a roof of the same material and was so low that the timbers

of the first story were laid above it. The water was supplied from
a well thirty feet deep in the east end of the basement.

> This font was built for the baptisms for the dead until the
> Temple shall be finished, when a more durable one will [take] its
> place. (*HC,* 4:446)

On Monday, the 8ᵗʰ of November, 1841, Joseph attended the
dedication of the baptismal font, in the Lord's House. Brigham Young
offered the dedicatory prayer.

This was the beginning of the great latter-day mission of The
Church of Jesus Christ of Latter-day Saints, to open the way for
baptism for the dead, by proxy, as referred to in the New Testament.
In the year of 1841, hundreds of Saints would afford themselves of
the privilege of being baptized for their loved ones. Emma would be
among them, receiving baptism for her mother and sister.

Some of the most sublime prose existing in latter-day scripture,
derived from Joseph's recording of the revelations he received
concerning this doctrine, are now found in several verses of sections
127 and 128 of the Doctrine and Covenants.

> Now, what do we hear in the gospel which we have received?
> A voice of gladness! A voice of mercy from heaven; and a voice of
> truth out of the earth; glad tidings for the dead; a voice of glad-
> ness for the living and the dead; glad tidings of great joy. How
> beautiful upon the mountains are the feet of those that bring glad
> tidings of good things. . . . (Doctrine and Covenants 128:19)

The year 1841 had been a grim year, with many Saints suffering
illness and death.

Some miraculous healings were performed through the laying on
of hands and ministration of priesthood blessings. Even so, sickness
and death stalked the Saints. By August, it had taken take its toll on
the members of the Smith family.

Joseph's brother, Don Carlos, then editor for the Church newspaper, *Times and Seasons,* died suddenly on August 7ᵗʰ. The entire community mourned his passing. Eight days later, Joseph and Emma's fourteen-month-old son, Don Carlos, died, on August 15ᵗʰ. In Joseph's *History of the Church,* mention of the death and burial of this baby is sandwiched between the meetings with the brethren, a visit by a group of Sac and Fox Indians, and Church conference meetings. Brigham Young took charge of the Conference, on account of the death of the baby. At noon, all of the Apostles who were in town for the Conference went together "to visit President Joseph Smith to comfort him in his afflictions" *(HC,* 2:403).

Despite the crushing sorrow in his household, during the afternoon Joseph attended the conference where he said the time had come when "the Twelve should be called upon to stand in their place next to the First Presidency. . ." *(HC,* 4:403). Specifically at this time the Twelve were to oversee the settling of immigrants and "the business of the Church at the stakes, and assist to bear off the kingdom victoriously to the nations. . . ." (ibid.). Joseph wanted very much to be able to spend more of his time attending "to the business of translating" (ibid.). Apparently his desire to accomplish this was thwarted by the heavy workload that filled the rest of the year. Nevertheless, Joseph continued to press forward preparing the baptismal font that was required in order for the Saints to perform vicarious baptism for their dead relatives who had not had a chance to receive the gospel in this life. His activities in this regard have already been described.

How did Joseph and Emma spend these traditional holidays this year? It is interesting to note that the day before Christmas shows Joseph engaged in administrative meetings, calling missionaries to various parts of the world, setting up of business projects, and detailing plans for establishing an agency in England for the "cheap and expeditious conveyance of the Saints to Nauvoo" *(HC,* 4:484).

Joseph and Emma's house must have been buzzing with activity. The Prophet and his wife lived in the same building of squared-off logs they had moved into upon their arrival at Nauvoo, and despite the recent addition, their home was none too commodious. Although Joseph now had an office in the nearly completed brick store, Emma would have been at work overseeing the constant demand for food to assuage the appetites of the many visitors who laid claim to her husband's time and attention.

At this time, Joseph was also making every effort to obtain goods for the store that he hoped to open as soon as it was stocked. The goods he had ordered from New Orleans were stopped, in St. Louis, by an individual who wanted to prevent Joseph from opening his store. To get around this deviltry, Joseph sent men and wagons to obtain what they could from other sources, but the store could not be opened until the New Year 1842.

Christmas Day 1841 came on Saturday. A party was held at the home of Hyrum Kimball. Brigham Young, Heber C. Kimball, Orson Pratt, Wilford Woodruff, John Taylor, and their wives were in attendance. No mention is made of Joseph and Emma being there. In fact, there is no mention of Joseph and Emma entertaining or holding either Christmas or New Year's Eve celebrations for the year of 1841. Since Emma was pregnant, perhaps she was not feeling up to entertaining. Even so, her house was the center of a great deal of activity.

All through the week before and after Christmas, Joseph's days were filled with civic and business and Church duties. On Sunday, the day after Christmas, Joseph and Emma opened their home for a public meeting at which Brigham Young, Patriarch Hyrum Smith, and Joseph addressed the congregation. Joseph read the thirteenth chapter of 1 Corinthians, and also part of the fourteenth chapter. He remarked that the gift of tongues was necessary in the Church, but warned that the devil could tempt people of any nationality or language. "The gift of tongues by the power of the Holy Ghost in the Church, is for the benefit of the servants of God to preach to unbelievers, as on the day of Pentecost," he said. He clarified the purpose for this gift, giving important instructions to the brethren regarding it *(HC,* 4:485-86).

In spite of the other pressing business at hand, Joseph himself took time on Tuesday, December 28th, to baptize Sidney Rigdon, Reynolds Cahoon and others, in the font, for their dead relatives *(HC,* 4:486).

As the year 1841 came to a close, notwithstanding the persistent harassment by those who misjudged and feared the rise of the Church, the Saints received understanding of the importance of assisting the European converts to gather to Nauvoo. Prophet Joseph's persistent efforts to build the baptismal font, and his urgency to clarify the priceless gift of baptism for the dead, was a soul-stirring message, and the Saints hearkened to his words. This priceless gift gave to the Church members power to serve their loved ones who depart this life without having the opportunity to be baptized.

1842

The Gift of Trust in God

On New Year's Day 1842, Joseph began putting goods on the shelves in the store that would become famous. The Red Brick Store (so named in our day, because its outer walls are made of red brick and its inner walls are painted a rustic dark red color) was to fulfill a dual purpose. It would serve as a place of business, where the public could obtain a wide variety of necessities—from cloth, shoes, tools, to molasses, flour, candles, and sundry other items of usefulness—and also as a sanctuary, where numerous sacred events would be enacted.

Engrossed as he was with opening his store, Joseph took time to comfort his wife, who gave birth to a stillborn son on February 6th. This sad occasion is recorded in Emma's handwriting in Emma and Joseph's family Bible (in possession of Buddy Youngreen, Orem, Utah).

Emma had barely recovered when she was elected president of the Relief Society of Nauvoo, on March 17th. When Joseph organized the Relief Society for the women of the Church, he told the small group gathered in the upper room of the store that the Church was not fully organized until the women were thus organized. Emma's election as president was a direct fulfillment of the promises made to her in the revelation given to her in 1830 (Doctrine and Covenants section 25).

Nauvoo was thriving. But the political climate of the country was boiling with controversy over issues such as slavery, taxation and trade agreements, and states rights. At first, many politicians in Illinois courted the Mormon vote, recognizing that the Mormons represented a potential power in the ballot box. On the other hand, there were some with opposing values regarding slavery (the Saints were against it) who sought to spread rumors against the Church and against Joseph personally, in order to stir up public opinion against the Church.

Notwithstanding the security provided by the Nauvoo City charter and the Nauvoo Legion of several thousand men, Joseph's life was in extreme danger throughout most of the summer.

In August, Emma wrote a beautifully worded letter to the governor of Illinois, pleading Joseph's case. She and Eliza R. Snow even visited him, in hopes of making him see the injustice of what was growing into a heated attack on the rights of the citizens of Nauvoo. The governor expressed astonishment at the judgment and talent manifest in the manner of Emma's address, but he refused to extend any help.

Joseph was forced into hiding for weeks at a time, to escape the bounty hunters sent from Missouri. At one point he sneaked into his own house under cover of darkness in order to give his sick wife and children blessings, then went back to his lonely hiding place on an island in the Mississippi. Emma visited him there, which brought him much comfort.

During many trying months, he could be home and safe only through the constant vigilance of his faithful bodyguards. But when he was left in peace, frequently we find that Joseph was engaged in doing household chores and chopping and bringing wood. So it was on December 13th, 1842.

On Christmas Eve he was "at home" reading, and revising his history with Willard Richards (his clerk), and visiting the sick; on Christmas Day, which was a Sunday, he was with his family and the Saints. The day after Christmas he proceeded with his duties as Justice of the Peace, and visited a sick sister. Returning to his home, he found Emma extremely ill. Although current printings of Joseph

Smith's history state that Emma bore a stillborn son on this date, this was an error undoubtedly caused by someone interpreting the word "chill" as "child," and embellishing the record to indicate she had a stillborn son *(HC,* 5:209). Subsequent research has shown her to have been sick with a chill at Christmas. Her stillborn child was born the previous February (Jones, "Finding the Testimony of My Great-Great Grandmother," *Ensign,* p. 34).

Sick though Emma was, Joseph could not stay at home with her. At 9:00 a.m. the next day, he left for Springfield, Illinois, for the hearing that would decide his fate on the Missouri extradition. This order was based on a false charge that he had attempted to murder Governor Lilburn Boggs, which he could prove he had not done. With such horrendous events hanging over them, Emma may have become ill due to overtaxed nerves. Without question, it would have been impossible to enjoy the holidays under these circumstances, with the fear and uncertainty concerning the outcome of the upcoming trial.

The weather was extremely cold as Joseph and a number of the brethren traveled to Springfield together. They then spent the remainder of the week preparing for the hearing. Joseph slept either on the floor or a couch at Judge Adam's home. His brothers Hyrum and William (William was a member of the legislature) stayed in Springfield with him. Thus surrounded with friends, the Prophet enjoyed several evenings of conversation concerning gospel principles.

New Year's Eve was spent taking care of the legal detail pertaining to the case against Joseph. He submitted to all that was required and endured ignoble treatment at the hands of rowdy men bent on making trouble. Because of the careful effort of the Marshall, Mr. Prentice, peace was obtained.

Joseph and his friends dined at the American House for lunch, then returned to Judge Adams' where they spent the closing hours of 1843.

Afterward, Joseph remarked, regarding his many afflictions: "[The] perils which I am called to pass through, they seem but a small thing to me, as the envy and wrath of man have been my common lot all the days of my life; and for what cause it seems mysterious, unless I was ordained from before the foundation of the world for some good end, or bad, as you may choose to call it. Judge ye for yourselves. God knoweth all these things, whether it be good or bad" (Doctrine and Covenants 127:2).

His willingness to accept and endure whatever happened, trusting in God, acknowledging the Lord's hand in all things, was a priceless example to the Church in his day, one that remains to this day.

1843

The Gift of Sealing Ordinances

Joseph returned to Nauvoo, from Springfield, a week before his and Emma's sixteenth wedding anniversary. He brought the happy news that he had been cleared of all charges, and was free to pursue his life without anxiety. This put them in a mood to celebrate.

Joseph and Emma sent invitations to all their friends, including the twelve apostles, the city council, their wives and children, to come to dinner on January 18th.

The event was reported in the *Times and Seasons:* "Mr. Smith and his lady made a feast and invited upwards to fifty of their friends to partake with them; which was indeed a day of conviviality and rejoicing, and might properly be called a day of jubilee or release" *(Times and Seasons* 4:96).

Of the celebration, Joseph wrote, "My home was small [they were still living in the old homestead] so but few could be accommodated at the time. Twenty-one sat down to the first table; twenty sat down to the second table; 18 at the third, among them were myself and Emma; and 15 at the fourth table including children and my household" *(HC,* 5:253).

Joseph said the day ". . . passed off pleasantly with many interesting anecdotes related by the company . . . who were very cheerful" (ibid.). The company sang, laughed, and feasted, enjoying a rare occasion of pure enthusiastic sociality.

Saints were coming from Europe in great numbers. Managing Nauvoo, as the melting pot of the Church, was a constant challenge to the Prophet, but more challenging still was the rising spirit of hatefulness from politicians who felt frustrated at being unable to control the political and social power of so large a number of united people in their county and state.

Although Joseph had been warned by Governor Ford not to involve himself in politics, he was elected mayor of Nauvoo. A natural leader, Joseph was one time asked how he governed so diverse and numerous a people. He stated he taught them correct principles and they governed themselves (*Journal of Discourses*, 10:57-58).

Notwithstanding all that was happening in business, politics, and socially, Joseph was continuing to open the understanding of his brethren to the magnificent work of the restored gospel. Two building projects, besides the temple, were in the making. One was to be a new home for Joseph and Emma and their growing family. The other was a foundation for a great hotel where the prophet hoped to entertain the great men of the earth.

On May 28th, Joseph asked his beloved brother Hyrum to perform the sealing ordinance for Emma and himself. This ordinance would seal them together as husband and wife for eternity. According to Brigham Young, who was there, the sealing was performed in the upstairs room of the old homestead.

In June the family tried to take a trip, but harassment by Missourians bent on kidnapping the prophet spoiled the only vacation they ever attempted. Emma's sister and several other of her relatives had moved to Illinois. With the plan of visiting these relatives, they set out in their buggy, for Dixon, Illinois. They had barely arrived at her sister's house when Joseph was abducted by Missourians, who hoped to take him across into Missouri, before his friends could rescue him. Emma and the children left right away to return to Nauvoo. What anxiety she must have endured before she knew Joseph had escaped and was safe. But when he was rescued by his loyal friends in the Nauvoo Legion and returned home to Nauvoo, she was there to greet him. It must have seemed like a holiday to them as she rode out on horseback to meet him. He embraced her and they rode back into town accompanied by the brass band and drum.

Emma turned 40, on July 10th. No notice is made of any birthday celebrations for her or the children, though they must surely have had family celebrations all through the years.

In July 1843, Joseph worried that he would not live long enough to see the temple finished and to be able to bestow vital priesthood ordinances to the Church. Since 1841, with this concern in mind, he had begun steadily to lay more and more responsibility upon the shoulders of the twelve apostles.

The last week of August Joseph moved his family into the Mansion House. It was a well-appointed house, adequate for the family. Because they could no longer afford to give free hospitality to so many guests, it became the Nauvoo Hotel. They added a large section on the back with a public dining room on the main floor, hotel rooms upstairs, and a basement for storage. While Emma took on the task of furnishing and decorating, Joseph continued his Church and civic duties.

Evidently aware that time was short, Joseph proceeded with the restoration of the fullness of priesthood ordinances. In September, he administered sacred ordinances to Emma in the upstairs front room of the Mansion House. Emma was the first woman to be so blessed. Under Joseph's direction, she later administered the same to many other women. This is one of the most priceless gifts to this dispensation, which comes to us through Emma. During a special endowment meeting, Joseph and Emma were the first couple to receive their calling and election made sure. These ordinances were administered by Hyrum Smith, a co-president of the Church, and William Marks, then Stake President in Navuoo. Joseph explained during this meeting that no more sacred ordinances can be conferred in mortality and that through this restoration, the foundation was complete.

The restoration of all these ordinances provided the means for all the faithful to someday obtain the fulness of priesthood blessing, when they have proven worthy. As the Bible indicates that which is sealed on earth will be sealed in heaven—death will never separate those who are thus joined by the power of the holy priesthood.

Thanks to the Prophet's perseverance, in spite of obstacles that would have discouraged others, this priceless gift, the sealing power, has been established upon the earth in the last days. It pertains to the principle referred to by the Apostle Paul when he declared, "Neither is the man without the woman; Neither is the woman without the man in the Lord" (1 Cor. 11:11-12). Only through the revelations of Joseph Smith can we fully understand the obscure Biblical passages that refer to the special authority resting on those holding the priesthood, to bind (or seal) on earth and in heaven.

This holiday season would be the last Joseph and Emma would have together in mortality. Joseph's history records that on December 23rd, which was his 38th birthday, he was "at home making preparations for a Christmas Dinner party" *(HC,* 6:133).

On Christmas Eve Joseph was at home and the Smiths received company. After they had retired for the night (about one in the morning on Christmas Day), they were awakened by a group of people singing under their window. Joseph recorded the names of these Christmas carolers, and tells of his activities for that Christmas Day.

> I was aroused by an English sister, Lettice Rushton, widow of Richard Rushton, Sr., (who ten years ago lost her sight,) accompanied by three of her sons, with their wives and her two daughters, with their husbands, and several of her neighbors,

singing, "Mortals, awake! With angels join," etc., which caused a
thrill of pleasure to run through my soul.

All my family and boarders arose to hear the serenade, and I
felt to thank my Heavenly Father for their visit, and blessed them
in the name of the Lord. They also visited my brother Hyrum,
who was awakened from his sleep. He arose and went out of
doors. He shook hands with and blessed each one of them in the
name of the Lord, and said that he thought at first that a cohort
of angels had come to visit him. (Ibid., 6:134)

Joseph and Emma entertained guests the entire day and evening.
Joseph wrote:

At two o'clock, about fifty couples sat down to my table to
dine. While I was eating, my scribe called, requesting me to
solemnize the marriage of his brother, Dr. Levi Richards, and
Sarah Griffiths; but as I could not leave, I referred him to
President Brigham Young, who married them.

A large party supped at my house, and spent the evening in
music, dancing, etc., in a most cheerful and friendly manner.
During the festivities, a man with his hair long and falling over
his shoulders, and apparently drunk, came in and acted like a
Missourian. I requested the captain of the police to put him out
of doors. A scuffle ensued . . . when, to my great surprise and joy
untold, I discovered it was my long-tried, warm, but cruelly
persecuted friend, Orrin Porter Rockwell, just arrived from
nearly a year's imprisonment, without conviction, in Missouri.
(Ibid.)

For another interesting viewpoint of this event, we look through
the eyes of a child, Joseph F. Smith, who was only about four or five
years old at the time. In his book *Joseph Smith the Prophet,* Preston
Nibley states:

In September, 1906, I visited Nauvoo in company with my
father and President Joseph F. Smith. Standing in the front room
of the Prophet's old home, President Joseph F. Smith told us that

he was present at this Christmas party in 1843. "My mother brought me and sat me down on the fiddler's platform in the corner of this very room," he said. He then related that while the dancing was going on, he noted the confusion caused by a man trying to get in at the door. He [the young Joseph F. Smith] saw the Prophet make his way through the crowd and take the man to his heart. (Corbett, *Mary Fielding Smith: Daughter of Britain*, p. 140)

From this we now know that Mary Fielding Smith and Hyrum were present on this occasion, and undoubtedly other children attended this party as well. Apparently the gathering was one of family and close friends, rather than an official Church gathering.

The year closed with Emma and Joseph making a New Year's visit to the home of their longtime friends, Parley P. Pratt and his wife. Since it was Sunday, "at early candle-light" they all went to a prayer meeting, where Joseph administered the sacrament.

It had been a momentous year of accomplishment in spite of trouble. Joseph and Emma had received, during this year, the sacred ordinances of eternal sealing, laying the foundation for future blessings, when the temples would dot the land and millions would be able to enter the houses of the Lord to receive their endowments. Through these difficult times, the priceless gift of sealing ordinances was given, which opens the way for all families to be together forever.

1844

The Priceless Gift of Love

The Prophet and Emma had much to be thankful for as they retired on New Year's Eve 1843. It was rainy, but warm. It was one of those years when there was no ice on the river. It seems appropriate that on this last New Year's Eve of Joseph's life, he was serenaded by a group singing a hymn written by William Phelps. At midnight, about fifty musicians and singers gathered under their window and sang "Phelps' New Year's Hymn."

William Phelps had gone through severe trials, and for a time had lost his faith and membership in the Church. He had regained his membership through sincere repentance. This man profoundly loved the restored gospel and the Prophet, and before another year had passed, he would preach the funeral sermon for his martyred friend. His faith found expression in prose, which ultimately became hymns. To this day, Saints everywhere thrill as they sing, "Praise to the Man" and more than a dozen other hymns extolling the message, and the messenger through whom the restoration was accomplished.

On New Year's Day, which was a Monday, the weather turned cold. That night there was a large party in the hotel dining room, with dancing till the wee hours of the morning. However, Joseph and his family, Elder John Taylor, and other friends, spent some quiet time together in their parlor.

Joseph spent the day of his wedding anniversary writing letters and attending to visitors. He mentions in passing that there was a party at the Mansion that evening, although whether he and Emma attended is not clear.

During the general conference on April 6th, a wonderfully large assembly heard the brethren preach. One particularly interesting speech, given by the Church patriarch, Hyrum Smith, touched on the importance of the Nauvoo Temple.

> . . . I want to get the roof on this season. I want to get the windows in, in the winter, so that we may be able to dedicate the House of the Lord by this time next year, if nothing more than one room. . . . I cannot make a comparison between the House of God and anything now in existence. Great things are to grow out of that house. There is a great and mighty power to grow out of it. There is an endowment. Knowledge is power. We want knowledge. . . . (*HC*, 5:300)

The kind of knowledge being referred to here is not of the world, but is the only knowledge that can save and exalt mankind: "This is life eternal, that ye might know God, the Eternal Father, and Jesus Christ. . . ." (John 17:3). The Prophet's message to the world was that we not only *can* know who and what we worship, we *must* know, or we cannot possibly serve God in light and truth and love him with all our hearts.

The Prophet's final months unfolded in an ever more intense teaching of the brethren and sisters of the Church, both in public and private. Joseph preached at the stand on the temple grounds, from his doorstep, and on the *Maid of Iowa* (a riverboat). Wherever a crowd gathered, asking questions, seeking counsel, he would be found, teaching as long as his voice would hold out.

Emma was also busy caring for the children and overseeing the management of the hotel. Earlier, in 1843, she had traveled to St. Louis to obtain dishes, bedding, furnishings, curtains, and other items for the hotel.

Many converts arrived on the boats that came upriver from New Orleans. These converts came primarily from Europe, England, and Scandinavia to make for themselves a new home in the thriving city of Nauvoo. Businesses prospered, and the temple drew many sight-seers as it rose gloriously.

An election year, with the pulse of antagonism again rising against the Mormons, could bring good or ill upon the community of Saints. One time when Emma prepared one of her specialty desserts, a kind of deep-fried scone served with sugar and cream, she was asked what it was called. She replied, "In an election year such as this is, they are called candidates, all puffed up and air in them" (Youngreen, *Reflections of Emma*, p. 104-105).

One might wonder if she was speaking of all politicians generally, or if she was perhaps teasing her husband, who was at the time a candidate for the U.S. presidency.

But, in the spring of 1844, Emma had another concern. She was expecting her ninth child. So far, only three of her babies had survived their birth. She had to guard her health, as she was no longer a young woman.

When Joseph found himself challenged with more litigation, he realized his enemies were not going to let him live in peace. Bent on tearing down the Nauvoo Charter, they were determined to dismantle the structure of freedom he had worked so hard to establish. In short, there was clearly a movement afoot to drive the Mormons out of the country.

Prophetically, Joseph told his close associates that the time would come when the Church would go to the Rocky Mountains and become a great people. He indicated he did not expect to be able to live long enough to go with them. But he had armed them with the gift of prophecy and all the authority they would require to carry on when he was gone.

As he rode out of the city, he returned home twice to say goodbye to his family. Passing through the beautiful city of Nauvoo, on his way to Carthage, he told his friends, "I am going like a lamb to the slaughter; but I am calm as a summer's morning; I have a conscience void of offense towards God, and towards all men. I shall die innocent, and it shall yet be said of me—he was murdered in cold blood" (Doctrine and Covenants 135:4).

Although he counseled his older brother not to go with him, Hyrum refused to let him go alone. The two brothers died together in Carthage, Illinois, at the hands of assassins.

The testimony of these two men would remain, untarnished, having been sealed with their blood. Their testimony remains, a bold statement to the world: God has restored his Church, he has revealed himself anew, and he has established prophets in the land. Though the enemies of truth killed the prophets, as they had in times of old, they could not kill the work. God had established the pattern and restored the gifts and powers of salvation, through the Prophet Joseph Smith. The priesthood will never be taken again from the earth, and all that has been promised through the holy scriptures shall be fulfilled.

At Joseph's funeral, William Phelps said, "The revelations he brought forth are everlasting witnesses that he, like the Savior, came not 'to drink and be merry, for tomorrow we die,' but to point out the way of life, and call upon all men to repent and be saved" (LDS Church Archives; see also Phelps, "The Joseph/Hyrum Smith Funeral Sermon," *BYU Studies,* Winter 1983, pp. 11-12).

"Greater love hath no man than this, that a man lay down his life for his friends." (John 15:12)

EPILOGUE

The Prophet Joseph Smith was killed by a mob of about 200 men, in Carthage, Illinois, on June 27, 1844. He would have been 39 on his next birthday. He left behind his pregnant wife, Emma, with her adopted daughter, Julia, and three sons, Joseph III, 11; Frederick, 8; and Alexander Hale, 6. He had asked Emma to name the unborn child David Hyrum, if it was a boy. This son was born on the 17th of November, 1844.

The Prophet's brother, Hyrum, also killed at Carthage, left behind his wife, Mary Fielding Smith, and her two little ones, Joseph (6) and Martha (3). Hyrum's eldest daughter, Lovina, married to Loren Walker, remained in Nauvoo to help Emma, but Hyrum's son, John, and two daughters, Jerusha and Sarah, went west with their stepmother.

Emma would not go west.

As Joseph was leaving the Mansion House before going to Carthage, he said to Emma, "Can you raise my sons to walk in their father's footsteps?"

She replied, "Joseph, you're coming back."

Again he repeated the question and she again replied, "You're coming back!"

And a third time, he asked, "Emma, can you raise my sons to walk in their father's footsteps?"

In response, she broke down and wept, saying, "Joseph, you are coming back!" (Newell and Avery, *Mormon Enigma: Emma Hale Smith*, p. 190).

When news came to her of his death, she was devastated. She exclaimed, "Why, O God, am I thus afflicted? Why am I a widow and my children orphans? Thou knowest I have always trusted in thy law." When a friend tried to comfort her by reminding her that this affliction would be to her a crown of life, she answered, "My husband was my crown; for him and for my children I have suffered the loss of all things; and why, O god, am I thus deserted, and my bosom torn with this ten-fold anguish?" (McGavin, *Nauvoo the Beautiful*, p. 144).

By all accounts, Emma did not easily recover from her sorrow. But she learned to live again, largely due to the need to take care of her little ones. They became her life.

Emma lived in Nauvoo another thirty-five years, and died there on April 30, 1879, at the age of seventy-four. After her remarriage in 1847, to Louis C. Bidamon, she continued to take in many other motherless children, including her daughter-in-law, Elizabeth Agnes Kendall, to whom she gave tender motherly attention and love.

At a memorial service held several months after her funeral, Mark H. Forscutt, paid her fine tribute:

> Was it not her loving hand, her consoling and comforting words, unswerving integrity, fidelity, and devotion, her wise counsel, that assisted to make this latter-day work a success? If God raised up a Joseph as a prophet and a restorer of gospel truth, then did he also raise up an Emma as a helpmeet for him." (Mark Forscutt, Tribute to Emma Smith Bidamon, RLDS Archives)

According to my great-grandfather, Alexander, who was with her when she died, Emma had a vision, or dream, shortly before her passing. She said Joseph came to her and took her into a beautiful mansion. As they passed through the apartments, she saw an infant, in a cradle, whom she recognized as her baby, Don Carlos, who had died in 1841. With great excitement she clasped the baby to her bosom. She turned to her husband and asked, "Joseph! Where are the rest of my children?" He replied, "Be patient, Emma, and you shall have all of your children" (Alexander Hale Smith, Sermon at Bottineau, N.D., given July 1, 1903).

In telling this story, Alexander reported that she also saw, "a personage of light, even the Lord Jesus Christ" (ibid.).

Thus, at her death, the promises were fulfilled that had been given in her patriarchal blessing, given in 1834: "Thou shalt see many days, yea, the Lord will spare thee until thou art satisfied, for thou shalt see thy Redeemer. Thy heart shalt rejoice in the great work of the Lord, and no one shall take thy rejoicing from thee."

For me, learning what happened when Emma died has been another priceless gift. It is her witness that families will surely be together in the hereafter.

After visiting the homes that have been preserved in Nauvoo, I suddenly recognized another priceless gift—one that has only been made possible because of her remaining in Nauvoo. The buildings Emma and Joseph once called home—the tiny log homestead, with its added-on rooms, the beautiful Mansion House, the red brick Nauvoo House, where Emma left her last testimony just before she died—all these homes have been preserved by the continued care of her descendants. Had Emma left Nauvoo, these homes would have undoubtedly passed into ruin.

Today literally millions of visitors pass through the rooms each year. I cannot help but think, when I go there, of the Christmases celebrated within those walls, some in peace, others in joy, some in pensive concern, but certainly all were spent reverently, in recognition of the great gifts the Savior's birth brings to mankind.

Between Emma and Me

written by Gracia N. Jones

Emma,

Between you and me,

What an example you are,

Both in your successes

And your failures.

In the holy temple

I think of you

and your role in making

The blessings I enjoy therein

Available.

In Relief Society,

I contemplate the dues you paid

For me,

That I may learn

of Charity.

At home,

I consider my duty,

And care more for it

Than acclamation

Of the world.

Like you,
I chafe against oppression,
Struggle with challenges;
Seek comfort
From our Savior.

We two,
Flawed mortals that we are;
With hearts contrite
And broken, Rejoice!

About the Author

I am a convert to the LDS church, as well as a great-great-grand-daughter of Joseph and Emma Smith. My husband, C. Ivor Jones, and I live in St. George, Utah. I am the mother of eight children and the grandmother of thirty-three.

Because my great-great-grandmother Emma did not go west with the Church after Joseph's death, Emma and Joseph's children were not raised in the LDS Church. For a century the descendants of the Lord's latter-day prophet were scattered, confused, and largely disconnected from knowledge of their heritage.

I joined the Church in 1956. I am the third descendant of Joseph and Emma to be baptized into the Church; I am the first to remain active. The first was Joseph III, who was baptized by his father, when he was eight years old. The second was a granddaughter, Alice Frederica Smith, daughter of Frederick, who joined in 1914, but then renounced her action, then being baptized by her cousin into the RLDS Church the following year. She later renounced that religion as well.

My conversion came when I was barely eighteen years old. I was totally ignorant of either the heritage of my great-great-grandfather, or any of the doctrines he taught. We were instructed, as children, not to tell anyone we were related to Joseph Smith. This same prejudice is widespread among many branches of the family. I have learned that this attitude is not founded in shame; rather it comes from the fear of persecution which has dogged the family through the generations.

When I first heard the testimony of the missionaries, I experienced a burning knowledge that it was true. I ignored the family prejudice and joined the Church.

This burning testimony began when a young missionary placed a little black book, with a gold picture embossed on the front, in my hands. He said, "This is the Book of Mormon. It was translated by the power of God, by your great-great-grandfather, and it is true."

As I took the book in my hands, I felt an overwhelming sense of enlightenment, a vibrating feeling that went from the top of my head down through my fingers and toes. My whole being was filled with *knowing:* "It is true. It is really true!"

I took the book home and began to read. I couldn't put it down. In view of the wonderful story and message, I kept wondering why the family had kept this a secret. I learned from my mother that as a child she was ridiculed because of her relationship to Joseph Smith. Because she knew very little about him, and nothing about the restored gospel, she could not defend herself. So she instructed her children not to tell anyone they were related to Joseph.

My relationship to Joseph and Emma comes through my mother, Lorena Horner Normandeau, who is the youngest daughter of Coral Cecil Rebecca Smith Horner, who was the youngest of Alexander Hale Smith's nine children. Alexander was the third of Joseph and Emma's four sons.

My grandfather, Louis H. Horner, was a farmer. He moved his family from Iowa to northwestern Montana in the 1930s. They settled near the town of Ronan, Montana, which is on the Flathead Indian Reservation. There my mother met Rupert A. Normandea while she was attending high school at Ronan.

My father's family came from Quebec, Canada, and his maternal great-grandfathers (Finley and Dubay) were living in the Flathead Valley in Montana by the mid-1800s.

Through my father, I am a member of the Flathead Indian Tribe, a heritage I consider significant. I have always appreciated my Indian heritage, more so after coming to know about the Book of Mormon, which tells about Father Lehi and his wife, Sariah, who are ancestors of the Indian people.

I have found it very interesting to learn that in the 1830s, about the same time that Joseph was sending missionaries to the Indians west in the area west of the Ohio River, members of the Flathead Indian Tribe sent a delegation to St. Louis to inquire whether someone would come to what is now Montana, to teach them the white man's ways. This delegation was killed before they arrived. A second delegation was sent; they died in St. Louis of smallpox, but the message spurred a missionary effort by both Protestants and Catholics.

Ironically, the persecution of the Saints at that time sidetracked the Church's missionary work to the Indians, and the LDS missionaries never reached the Flathead Indian Tribe during Joseph's lifetime. It would be many years before the Book of Mormon would reach the Flathead Valley of Montana.

I thrill when I realize that the promises given to the prophets of the Book of Mormon concerning the remnant of Lehi's descendants—that they would someday receive the record he had prepared—is in some measure being fulfilled through my family.

It touches my heart to read that Hyrum's grandson, Joseph Fielding Smith, once said, "All my life I have prayed and hoped that the Lord would touch the hearts of the children of the Prophet Joseph Smith" (McGavin, *Joseph Smith's Family*, p. 282). I feel he would be pleased to know that the Prophet Joseph Smith now has many descendants in the LDS Church.

Six descendants have filled full-time missions, and a great "crop" is coming up as the young people are either filling missions or preparing to do so. Also, each year we learn of other family members, previously unknown to us, who have been baptized.

This book is my sincere effort to share my testimony and the truths I have learned concerning the work my ancestors performed and the priceless gifts that are now ours because of their efforts in restoring this sacred message.

The research I have done for this booklet has caused me deep feelings of gratitude for every convenience we enjoy today. I am also deeply grateful for friends and family, and my membership in the Church. I am especially thankful to finally learn about my great-great-grandfather, who was a prophet of God.

When I consider that he opened the dispensation of the fullness of times, which is spoken of in biblical prophecy, that he laid the foundation for the kingdom spoken of by the prophet Daniel, I thrill through and through.

To know that my ancestor saw the Father and Son in person and that the Lord Jesus Christ called him "friend" opens to my heart a new vista regarding the need for the hearts of the children to turn to their fathers. Through the Book of Mormon, and my activity in the LDS Church, the promises made to my forefathers, Lehi and Joseph Smith, have been planted in my heart. I know this is made possible through the power of the Holy Ghost. Indeed, the testimony I received when I was given the Book of Mormon has expanded, and I have come to know the real meaning of Christmas.

BIBLIOGRAPHY

Anderson, Richard Lloyd. *Investigating the Witnesses of the Book of Mormon.* Salt Lake City: Deseret Book, 1958.

Corbett, Don C. *Mary Fielding Smith: Daughter of Britain.* Salt Lake City: Deseret Book, 1995.

Faulring, Scott H., ed. *An American Prophet's Record—Diaries and Journals of Joseph Smith,* ed. Salt Lake City: Signature Books in Association with Smith Research Associates, 1987.

Forscutt, Mark. Tribute to Emma Smith Bidamon. 1879. RLDS Archives.

Hartley, William G. *My Best for the Kingdom: History and Autobiography of John Lowe Butler, A Mormon Frontiersman.* Salt Lake City: Aspen Book, 1993.

Jessee, Dean C., ed. *The Personal Writings of Joseph Smith.* Salt Lake City: Deseret Book, 1984.

Jones, Gracia N. *Emma's Glory and Sacrifice—A Testimony.* Hurricane, Utah: Homestead Publishers, 1987.

_____. "Finding the Testimony of My Great-Great-Grandmother, Emma Hale Smith," *Ensign,* August 1993, p. 30-39.

McGavin, E. Cecil. *Joseph Smith's Family.* Salt Lake City: Bookcraft, 1963.

_____. *Nauvoo the Beautiful.* Salt Lake City: Bookcraft, 1972.

Newell, Linda King, and Valeen Tippets Avery. *Mormon Enigma: Emma Hale Smith.* Garden City, New York: Doubleday & Co., 1984.

Nibley, Preston. *Brigham Young: The Man and His Work.* Salt Lake City, Utah: Deseret Book, 1936.

Pratt, Parley P. *Autobiography of Parley P. Pratt.* Salt Lake City: Deseret Book, 1966.

Smith, Alexander Hale. Sermon given at Bottineau, North Dakota on 1 July 1903. Printed in *Zion's Ensign*, December 31, 1903, Independence, Missouri.

Smith, Emma. "Emma Smith's Last Testimony," February 1879. RLDS Church Archives, Independence, Missouri.

Smith, Emma. Letters to Joseph (1837-1839). Copies in possession of author.

Smith, Joseph, Jr. *History of the Church of Jesus Christ of Latter-day Saints.* Salt Lake City: Deseret Book, 1974.

Smith, Joseph, Jr. Letters to Emma (1832-1840). Copies in possession of author.

Smith, Joseph III. *Memoirs of President Joseph Smith III—1832-1914.* Ed. Audentia Smith Anderson. Independence, Missouri: Harold Publishing House, 1979.

Smith, Lucy Mack. *History of Joseph Smith By His Mother, Lucy Mack Smith.* Preston Nibley, editor. Salt Lake City: Bookcraft, 1959.

_____. *The Revised and Enhanced History of Joseph Smith by His Mother*. Edited by Scot Facer Proctor and Maurine Jensen Proctor. Salt Lake City: Bookcraft, 1996.

Smith, Vida. *Story of Alexander Hale Smith*, Journal History, RLDS Church Archives. Copy in author's possession.

Whitney, Orson F. *Life of Heber C. Kimball: An Apostle, The Father and Founder of the British Mission*. Salt Lake City: Bookcraft, 1945.

Youngreen, Buddy. *Reflections of Emma*. Orem, Utah: Grandin Book Company, 1982.